Why Did Jesus Have to Die?

LEADER GUIDE

WHY DID JESUS HAVE TO DIE?
THE MEANING OF THE CRUCIFIXION

978-1-7910-4061-1
978-1-7910-4062-8 *eBook*
978-1-7910-4063-5 *Large Print*

DVD
978-1-7910-4066-6

Leader Guide
978-1-7910-4064-2
978-1-7910-4065-9 *eBook*

Also by Adam Hamilton

24 Hours That Changed the World	*John*	*Speaking Well*
Christianity and World Religions	*Leading Beyond the Walls*	*The Call*
Christianity's Family Tree	*Living Unafraid*	*The Journey*
Confronting the Controversies	*Love to Stay*	*The Lord's Prayer*
Creed	*Luke*	*The Message of Jesus*
Enough	*Making Sense of the Bible*	*The Walk*
Faithful	*Moses*	*The Way*
Final Words from the Cross	*Not a Silent Night*	*Unafraid*
Forgiveness	*Prepare the Way for the Lord*	*When Christians Get It Wrong*
Half Truths	*Revival*	*Wrestling with Doubt, Finding Faith*
Incarnation	*Seeing Gray in a World of Black and White*	*Words of Life*
	Simon Peter	*Why?*

For more information, visit AdamHamilton.com.

ADAM HAMILTON

WHY DID JESUS HAVE TO DIE?

THE MEANING OF THE CRUCIFIXION

LEADER GUIDE

Abingdon Press | Nashville

WHY DID JESUS HAVE TO DIE?

THE MEANING OF THE CRUCIFIXION

LEADER GUIDE

Copyright © 2025 Adam Hamilton

All rights reserved.

978-1-7910-4064-2

Cover art: Francisco de Zurbarán (Spanish, 1598–1664), *The Crucifixion*, 1627, Oil on canvas, Robert A. Waller Memorial Fund, The Art Institute of Chicago, Chicago, IL. Accession number 1954.1, https://www.artic.edu/artworks/80084/the-crucifixion.

Cover Description: The cover features a classical-style painting of Jesus on the cross. His head is bowed to one side, and he wears a white cloth around his waist. The background is dark, emphasizing the figure of Christ. At the top, gold serif text reads "Adam Hamilton," with smaller gold text beneath it saying "Author of *Creed, The Message of Jesus,* and *Wrestling with Doubt, Finding Faith.*" Large white serif text in the center asks, "Why Did Jesus Have to Die?" Below that, smaller gold text reads, "The Meaning of the Crucifixion." A red band at the bottom displays white text: "Leader Guide."

MANUFACTURED IN THE UNITED STATES OF AMERICA

CONTENTS

View a complimentary session
of Adam Hamilton's
Why Did Jesus Have to Die?

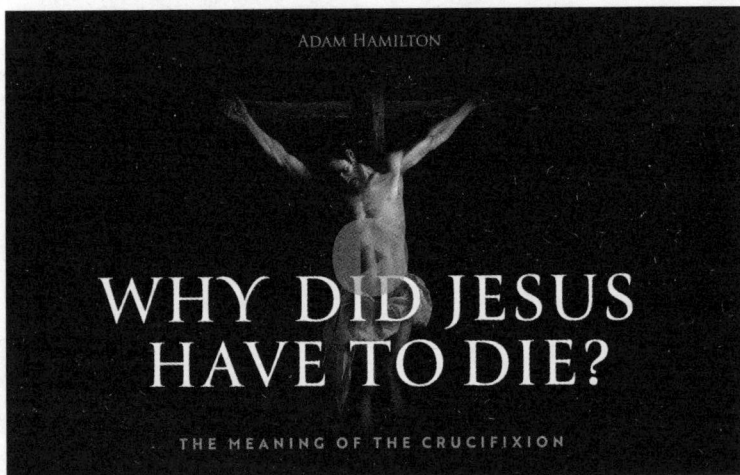

Scan the QR code below or visit
https: //bit.ly/whydidjesushavetodie.

INTRODUCTION

In *Why Did Jesus Have to Die?*, Adam Hamilton (senior pastor, Church of the Resurrection in Kansas City) offers insights into a question he has heard many Christians grapple with. They believe Jesus died for them but don't fully comprehend the reasons for or the full significance of his death.

Adam introduces readers to several theories about how Jesus' death brings us into a right relationship with God—the reality that in Christian doctrine is called the *atonement*. Rather than choose one single theory above all others or understand any of them as mechanical transactions, Adam argues these theories can complement each other and work together to give us a fuller and deeper understanding of why Jesus died and what his death means for us.

This leader guide can help you lead a group of adults in a study of Adam's book and the Scripture passages he discusses. Each of its six session plans corresponds to a chapter, named with a hymn title, in Adam's book:

- *Session 1: Lift High the Cross.* Drawing on the Gospel of
  John's proclamation of Jesus as the incarnate Word of
  God, this session encourages participants to think of the
  Crucifixion as God's embodied message to humanity. It also
  addresses historical reasons for Jesus' death and considers
  Jesus as a new "head" of the human race who reverses our
  primeval fall into sin.
- *Session 2: O Love Divine, What Thou Hast Done.* This session
  focuses on teachings from Romans, 2 Corinthians, and
  Hebrews to explore the idea that Jesus' death secures God's
  forgiveness of our sins as the just punishment for our sin and
  as a sacrificial offering of atonement.
- *Session 3: Agnus Dei.* Christian liturgy and art frequently
  depict Jesus as the Lamb of God. This session considers the

7

significance of that imagery by tracing its roots to the Jewish
celebration of Passover, examining how Jesus' death frees us
from captivity to sin.

- *Session 4: Were You There* In the first of two sessions, focused
  on the moral influence or moral example atonement theory,
  participants will consider how the emotional impact of Jesus'
  death can move us to live the life of loving service he lived,
  exemplified by his washing of his disciples' feet in John 13.
- *Session 5: What Wondrous Love Is This.* The second session
  focused on moral influence atonement theory considers Jesus'
  death as a self-sacrificial act of love, the kind of love to which
  Jesus calls his disciples in John 15.
- *Session 6: Love's Redeeming Work Is Done.* The final session
  introduces the *Christus Victor* theory of atonement, focusing
  on Jesus' death as a decisive victory over the powers of sin, evil,
  and death, as proclaimed in Hebrews 2 and 1 Corinthians 15.

Although this leader guide assumes all participants are reading Adam's
book, it includes quotations from the book and key Scripture passages so
that leaders can use it on its own. Additionally, the accompanying DVD
or streaming video from Amplify Media can supplement these session
plans.

Each session contains the following elements to draw from as you
plan six in-person, virtual, or hybrid sessions:

- *Session Objectives*
- *Biblical Foundations.* Key Scripture texts for each session,
  from the NRSV.
- *Before Your Session.* Tips to help you prepare a productive
  session.
- *Starting Your Session.* Discussion questions intended to warm
  up your group for fruitful discussion.

- *Opening Prayer.* Use the prayer as written or let it suggest a prayer in your own words.
- *Watch Session Video.* A prompt to play the appropriate track on the DVD or the streaming session of *Why Did Jesus Have to Die?*
- *Book Discussion Questions.* You likely will not be able or want to use all the questions in every session. Pick and choose questions based on your group's interests and the Spirit's leading.
- *Closing Your Session.* A discussion or reflection, usually focused on a specific quotation from Adam's book.
- *Closing Prayer.* Each session suggests using as a closing prayer the hymn after which Adam titled the corresponding book chapter.

Thank you for your willingness to lead! As a result of your study, may you and your group grow in your understanding of Jesus' death, and even more in your grateful response to and faithful service of our crucified and risen Lord.

Note: If pastors or groups begin the study on the first Sunday of Lent and complete all six sessions in order, the final session ("Christ the Lord Is Risen Today") will fall on Palm Sunday. Those who prefer to conclude on Easter Sunday may instead use the first week to discuss the book's preface and introduction, then begin session 1 ("Lift High the Cross") on the second Sunday of Lent. A session plan for the preface and introduction is available through the QR code below or by visiting https://bit.ly/wdjhtd_leaderhelps.

SESSION 1

LIFT HIGH THE CROSS

Session Objectives

This session will help participants:

- Consider how images of Jesus' crucifixion are like and unlike influential historical photographs.
- Offer their own, initial responses to the question "Why did Jesus have to die?"
- Review and reflect on evidence from the Gospels about the historical reasons behind Jesus' death.
- Contemplate the Crucifixion as a message from God, using John 1:18 as background.
- Consider the recapitulation theory of the atonement, exploring its seeds in the apostle Paul's letters.
- Plan one specific way to embody a prayer for God's will to be done through them.

Biblical Foundations

*In the beginning was the Word
    and the Word was with God
    and the Word was God.
The Word was with God in the beginning.
Everything came into being through the Word,
    and without the Word
    nothing came into being.
What came into being
    through the Word was life,
    and the life was the light for all people.
The light shines in the darkness,
    and the darkness doesn't extinguish the light....*

*The Word became flesh
    and made his home among us.
We have seen his glory,
    glory like that of a father's only son,
        full of grace and truth*

(John 1:1-5, 14)

Just as through one human being sin came into the world, and death came through sin, so death has come to everyone, since everyone has sinned. Although sin was in the world, since there was no Law, it wasn't taken into account until the Law came. But death ruled from Adam until Moses, even over those who didn't sin in the same way Adam did—Adam was a type of the one who was coming.

But the free gift of Christ isn't like Adam's failure. If many people died through what one person did wrong, God's grace is multiplied even more for many people with the gift—of the one person Jesus Christ—that comes through grace. The gift isn't like the consequences of one person's sin. The judgment that came from one person's sin led to punishment, but the free gift that came out of many failures led to the verdict of acquittal. If death ruled because of one person's failure, those who receive the multiplied grace and the gift of righteousness will even more certainly rule in life through the one person Jesus Christ

(Romans 5:12-17)

11

Before Your Session

- Carefully and prayerfully read this session's Biblical Foundations more than once. Write down questions you have, and try to answer them, consulting trusted Bible commentaries.

- Carefully read the introduction and chapter 1 of *Why Did Jesus Have to Die?* more than once.

- You will need: Bibles for in-person participants (*optional*: of the same translation, for unison reading) and/or screen slides prepared with Scripture texts for sharing (identify the translation used); newsprint or a markerboard and markers (for in-person sessions); paper, pens or pencils (in-person).

- If using the DVD or streaming video, preview the session 1 video segment. Choose the best time in your session plan for viewing it.

- *Optional*: Choose some influential historical photographs to display, including the image of Peter, who escaped slavery, that Adam discusses in chapter 1.

Starting Your Session

Welcome participants. Express why you are enthusiastic about leading this study of *Why Did Jesus Have to Die?* by Adam Hamilton. Invite participants to talk briefly about what they hope to gain from the study.

Tell participants that in chapter 1 Adam reflects on the power of "some of the most influential photographs," images that can "change hearts and even the course of history." *Optional*: Display the influential historical photographs you selected before your session and discuss them with participants.

Discuss:

- What famous photographs would you nominate as "some of the most influential" in history and why? How might history be different without these images?
- Adam discusses a Civil War-era photograph of Peter, who escaped slavery and whose badly scarred back "became a portrait of the evils of slavery." What is the most powerful image of unjust suffering you have seen? How did it affect you? What, if anything, did and does it motivate you to do?
- How are images—visual images, word images, mental images—of Jesus' crucifixion like and unlike these influential historical photographs?
- What is the most powerful image of Jesus' crucifixion you know and why?
- How have and do images of Jesus' crucifixion "change hearts and even the course of history?"

Tell participants your group will be considering many "images" of Jesus' crucifixion—in other words, theories about its significance and explanations of its meaning—during your study. Read aloud from Adam's book: "In order to fully understand the cross, you need to see *all* of these." Adam compares this view to looking through a kaleidoscope, piecing together a puzzle, or creating a tile mosaic or stained glass window: "Each piece is only a part of the whole, and only when taken together do we begin to fully comprehend the power of the cross of Christ."

Opening Prayer

God Most High and Holy, your Son Jesus suffered death on a cross for us and our salvation. We stand in awe of this mystery—unable fully to understand or explain it, but overwhelmed with gratitude and moved to respond, imperfect though our response must be. As we seek greater insight into the saving power of Christ's death, may your Spirit reshape us more thoroughly into his image, that we may

13

*faithfully offer ourselves to you and to others, as he offered himself
for the life of the world. Amen.*

Watch Session Video

Watch the session 1 video segment together. Discuss:

- Which of Adam's statements most interested, intrigued,
surprised, or confused you? Why?
- What questions does this video segment raise for you?

Book Discussion Questions

Historical Reasons for Jesus' Death

Read aloud from Adam's book: "Neither the religious leaders nor the
Roman governing apparatus believed they were putting Jesus to death for
any saving purpose. Both were ridding themselves of a problem."

Form two groups of participants. Assign each group one of these sets
of Scripture passages to read and discuss. Participants should answer this
question (which you may want to write on newsprint or markerboard):
What do these Scriptures say about historical reasons for opposition to
Jesus?

Group One: Religious Leaders
- Mark 11:15-18
- Mark 14:55-65
- John 11:45-53

Group Two: Roman Government
- Mark 15:1-5
- Luke 23:1-5
- John 19:19-22

After allowing time for small group discussion, bring the two groups
together. Ask a volunteer from each to summarize their small group's
conversation. Discuss:

- Different authorities had different reasons for wanting Jesus' death. What common elements, if any, do you find in the opposition to Jesus?
- The Gospels were written several decades after Jesus' death as expressions of faith in Jesus and are not history or biography as we understand those genres today. How much can we trust the Gospels as records of historical reasons for Jesus' death? Why?
- Do you think the religious leaders and Roman authorities share equal responsibility for Jesus' death, or does one group bear more than the other? Why?
- John repeatedly refers to those first-century religious leaders who opposed Jesus as "the Jews." How can we read such references to Jesus' opponents today without perpetuating anti-Jewish stereotypes that have historically caused harm?
- Where and how have you seen opposition to Jesus from leaders in religion and government today?

Atonement

Tell participants that Christian faith is concerned with more than historical reasons for Jesus' death. In this study, you and your group will explore the theological reasons.

Tell participants the word *atonement* refers to the result of Jesus' death as it relates to sin and/or our relationship with God. As Adam explains, English Bible scholar and translator William Tyndale (born c. 1490, died 1536) apparently coined it to signify "what was necessary to be reconciled or made at one with God." Theories about how Christ's death makes us "at one" with God are called theories of the atonement.

Discuss:

- What does it mean for you to be "at one" with God?
- As Adam explains, the New Testament does not offer one, detailed theory of the atonement, but instead presents "a dozen different metaphors" and multiple "glimpses" of how Jesus' death accomplishes it. Why do you think this is so?

- If the New Testament does not contain atonement theories, do Christians need them? Why or why not?
- In a few words, how would you, at the beginning of our study, answer the question, Why did Jesus have to die?

The Crucifixion as God's Word

Have participants turn in their Bibles to John 1. Recruit a volunteer to read aloud John 1:1-18 (or at least 1:1-4, 14) as other participants read along silently. Discuss:

- Who is "the Word"? What does the Word do? What is the Word's relationship with God?
- Adam notes, "The Greek word for 'Word' here is Logos, which means not simply word, but message, speech, logic, reason, and more." What do these additional definitions of Logos add to your understanding of this Scripture passage?
- The Logos was an image familiar to first-century Jewish and Greek philosophers. How would you paraphrase this Scripture text in images and language your society would easily understand?
- Adam points out that, in Scripture, the "word of God" is "never merely a book, a written document, or a story." What do these verses show or tell us about God's word?: Genesis 1:1-3; Exodus 19:3-6; Isaiah 40:6-8; Jeremiah 20:7-9; Matthew 4:3-4; Ephesians 6:17; Hebrews 4:12-13.
- "Jesus embodies God's Word. His life is the visible Word of God." What, specifically, in Jesus' life communicates God's word to you? Why?
- "If we begin by seeing the Crucifixion and the atonement through the lens of John's prologue," suggests Adam, "then we can recognize that Jesus' death is not primarily a transaction, mechanism, or formula," but "is first and foremost *a Word or message* from God." What is the distinction Adam is drawing, and why does it matter?

- What is God saying or trying to say in and through the Crucifixion?

A Return to and Reversing of Eden

Invite one more volunteers to tell in their own words the story of the garden of Eden (found in Genesis 2:4b-3, to which participants may wish to refer). Discuss:

- What interests, surprises, or confuses you most about the story of Eden?
- Adam notes that some people read this story literally while others read it metaphorically. How do you read it, and why?
- "The point of the story is to tell us about ourselves," writes Adam. Adam and Eve's "story is humanity's story—our *defining* story." What does the story of Eden tell you about human beings? About yourself, specifically?

Have participants turn their Bibles to Romans 5. Invite a volunteer to read aloud Romans 5:12-17 as other participants read along silently. Discuss:

- What connections does the apostle Paul make between the story of Eden and the story of Jesus?
- Read 1 Corinthians 15:21-22, 45. What do these verses add to your understanding of the connections Paul makes between Adam and Jesus?
- Adam calls the idea Paul is teaching the recapitulation theory of the atonement: "Recapitulation . . . is literally to re-head something," and, "as an atonement theory, means to restate our story as humans, only now with a new head of the human race, no longer Adam, but Jesus." How does Jesus reverse and redefine humanity's story, according to Paul? In what sense is Jesus now "head of the human race"?

WHY DID JESUS HAVE TO DIE?: LEADER GUIDE

- Adam stresses that Jesus' prayer in Gethsemane before his death, "*thy* will be done" (see Matthew 26:36-46; Mark 14:32-42; Luke 22:39-46), is the opposite of how Adam and Eve might have prayed: "*my* will be done." When and how have you found yourself praying each of these prayers? What happened?

- Adam contrasts the tree of the knowledge of good and evil, from which Adam and Eve ate forbidden fruit, with the tree of life in the New Jerusalem, with leaves "for the healing of the nations" (Revelation 22:2). How does the recapitulation theory speak to the restoration symbolized by these two trees? How can and do Christians become a part of this restoration today?

- How helpful or meaningful do you find the recapitulation theory? Why?

Closing Your Session

Read aloud from Adam's book: "In this powerful redeeming and atoning story, which path will you take? Will you follow the first Adam or the Second? Will you pray with Adam, 'Not thy will, but *my* will be done'? Or will you pray with Jesus, 'Not my will, but *thy* will be done'?"

Give participants a brief time of silence to think and pray about one specific circumstance or relationship in which they want God to do God's will through them. After the silence, if desired, invite any who wish to briefly talk about their prayer with the group.

Closing Prayer

Sing or read aloud together "Lift High the Cross" (*The United Methodist Hymnal* #159; https://hymnary.org/text/come_christians _follow_where_our_savior) or another hymn or song related to this session's themes or Scripture.

Session 2

O Love Divine, What Hast Thou Done

Session Objectives

This session will help participants:

- Consider the definition of sin as "missing the mark" and articulate their own definitions of sin.
- Understand basic elements of penal substitutionary atonement theory and compare it with Paul's teachings about Jesus' death in Romans 6 and 2 Corinthians 5.
- Understand basic elements of sacrificial atoning offering theory, comparing it to the teaching about Jesus' death in the letter to the Hebrews.

Biblical Foundations

When you were slaves of sin, you were free from the control of righteousness. What consequences did you get from doing things that you are now ashamed of? The outcome of those things is death. But now that you have been set free from sin and become slaves to God, you have the consequence of a holy life, and the outcome is eternal life. The wages that sin pays are death, but God's gift is eternal life in Christ Jesus our Lord.

(Romans 6:20-23)

[Christ] died for the sake of all so that those who are alive should live not for themselves but for the one who died for them and was raised.

So then, from this point on we won't recognize people by human standards. Even though we used to know Christ by human standards, that isn't how we know him now. So then, if anyone is in Christ, that person is part of the new creation. The old things have gone away, and look, new things have arrived!

All of these new things are from God, who reconciled us to himself through Christ and who gave us the ministry of reconciliation. In other words, God was reconciling the world to himself through Christ, by not counting people's sins against them. He has trusted us with this message of reconciliation.

So we are ambassadors who represent Christ. God is negotiating with you through us. We beg you as Christ's representatives, "Be reconciled to God!" God caused the one who didn't know sin to be sin for our sake so that through him we could become the righteousness of God

(2 Corinthians 5:15-21)

We have been made holy by God's will through the offering of Jesus Christ's body once for all.

Every priest stands every day serving and offering the same sacrifices over and over, sacrifices that can never take away sins. But when this priest offered one sacrifice for sins for all time, he sat down at the right side of God. Since then, he's waiting until his enemies are made into a footstool for his feet, because he perfected the people who are being made holy with one offering for all time.

(Hebrews 10:10-14)

Before Your Session

- Carefully and prayerfully read this session's Biblical Foundations more than once. Write down questions you have, and try to answer them, consulting trusted Bible commentaries.

- Carefully read chapter 2 of *Why Did Jesus Have to Die?* more than once.
- You will need: Bibles for in-person participants (*optional*: of the same translation, for unison reading) and/or screen slides prepared with Scripture texts for sharing (identify the translation used); newsprint or a markerboard and markers (for in-person sessions); paper, pens or pencils (in-person).
- If using the DVD or streaming video, preview the session 2 video segment. Choose the best time in your session plan for viewing it.
- If meeting in person, prepare some simple game involving aiming at a target that participants can play (even as simple as throwing crumpled balls of paper into a wastebasket).

Starting Your Session

Welcome participants. If meeting in person, invite volunteers to play the simple aiming game you have prepared. (If you are conducting a hybrid or fully remote session, you can ask participants to try tossing something soft at an impromptu target where they are located.) Discuss:

- What (other) games or sports involve taking aim at a target? Which of these, if any, do you enjoy or not enjoy, and why?
- As Adam explains, the word for "sin" in New Testament Greek is *hamartia* and was originally used to describe an archer's arrow missing its mark. What is our mark or target in this image of sin? How helpful or unhelpful do you find this image? Why?
- How do you define sin? How did you arrive at this definition?
- Adam mentions the Seven Deadly Sins: gluttony, lust, greed, sloth (or indifference), wrath (or anger and hate), envy, and pride. Where have you seen evidence of one or more of these sins in current events or culture? Do you think other sins

belong on a list of "deadly sins?" If so, which ones, and why? If not, why not?

- Adam also quotes a prayer of confession that asks forgiveness for "what we have done"—sins of commission—and "what we have left undone"—sins of omission. Which kind of sin do you struggle with more? Why?

Remind participants the Bible does not "teach" any single atonement theory (or, indeed, any formal doctrine); rather, the several atonement theories seek to illuminate Scripture's varied claims about the meaning of Jesus' death. Tell participants that in this session, your group will explore two influential atonement theories and some of their scriptural bases.

Opening Prayer

O God, you alone are holy and good. We are people of unclean lips, and not one of us is worthy to enter your presence. Yet in mercy and love, you not only invite us but bring us before you, removing our guilt, blotting out our sin that we may serve you. As we seek to better understand how you pardon us in Christ's offering of his life, may we more fully trust that you have pardoned us. Keep us confident that we are holy as you are holy—not by anything we have done, but only by all you have done through your Spirit, and in the death and resurrection of your Son Jesus, our great High Priest. Amen.

Watch Session Video

Watch the session 2 video segment together. Discuss:

- Which of Adam's statements most interested, intrigued, surprised, or confused you? Why?
- What questions does this video segment raise for you?

Book Discussion Questions

Penal Substitutionary Atonement

Have participants turn in their Bibles to Romans. Recruit a volunteer to read aloud Romans 6:20-23. Discuss:

- What before-and-after, then-and-now difference does Paul claim his readers have experienced? What is the reason for this change? (Refer to 6:16-19 for more context.)
- Paul says death is the "consequences" or "wages" of sin (v. 23a). What does he mean? How, if at all, have you seen or experienced this consequence of sin?
- Does the fact that not all sins lead to physical death complicate or undermine Paul's assertion? Why or why not?
- Paul contrasts sin's wages of death with God's gift of "eternal life in Christ Jesus" (v. 23b). What does he say earlier in 6:1-11 about how we receive this gift?
- What practical difference does Paul say God's gift of eternal life should and does make in life now (see 6:12-15)?

Have participants turn in their Bibles to 2 Corinthians. Recruit a volunteer to read aloud 2 Corinthians 5:15-21. Discuss:

- In 2 Corinthians, Paul is defending himself and his ministry against attacks from those he sarcastically calls "super-apostles" (see 11:1-15; 12:1-10), who question his authority, claim superiority to him, and teach another message. How do Paul's claims in this passage reflect that situation?
- What does Paul say in this passage about the purpose of Jesus' death?
- What does Paul mean when he says God caused Jesus "to be sin" when he "knew no sin" (v. 21)?

- Paul says he no longer regards Jesus or anyone from "a human point of view" (v. 16, NRSV). What standards is he talking about? Why do these criteria no longer apply?
- Have you ever experienced a significant change in how you regard Jesus? If so, what was it and what prompted that change?
- How has your faith changed the way you regard other people? The way you regard yourself?
- Paul depicts his message as the "message of reconciliation" between God and people (vv. 19-20). Why did God and humanity need to be reconciled? Is this reconciliation fully accomplished, a work in progress, or both?

After discussing the Scripture passages, write this heading on newsprint or markerboard: "Penal Substitutionary Atonement." Briefly define these terms:

- *Atonement*: "to be reconciled or made at one with God" (see session 1)
- *Penal*: relating to penalties for criminal offenders; derived from Greek and Latin terms for pain and punishment
- *Substitution*: replacing one person or thing with another

Describe penal substitutionary atonement theory, following Adam's explanation below (you may wish to write notes on the newsprint or markerboard):

- God, who is just, is angered by sin.
- All humans have sinned and justly deserve death for it, both physical death and eternal separation from God.
- Because God loves humanity, God sent Jesus to suffer, in our place, the just punishment for sin that humanity deserves.
- Only Jesus, God incarnate, could bear the just punishment for sin.

Discuss:

- What does this theory tell us about God's justice? God's wrath? God's love?
- How well does this theory reflect Paul's teaching in Romans 6 and 2 Corinthian 15? Why?
- Is God just to punish the innocent Jesus for others' sin, as this theory holds? Why or why not?
- Adam asks, "Is it really true that God cannot forgive sin without punishment being meted out to someone?" What do you think?
- Do you think this atonement theory reflects Jesus' attitude toward sinners as seen in the Gospels? Why or why not?
- What implications, if any, does this atonement theory have for human approaches to justice, punishment, and forgiveness?

Sacrificial Atonement Offering

Read aloud from Adam's book: "The idea of making an offering to atone for our sins is not hard to understand." Ask:

- Have you ever offered something to atone for something wrong you've done? Has anyone ever made such an offering to you? What happened?
- Whom did God choose to serve as God's priests in the Law (Exodus 28:1; Leviticus 8:1-5)? What were these priests' duties (Exodus 29:35-46; Leviticus 9:1-7; Numbers 18:1-7)?
- How are the offerings and sacrifices God commanded a reflection of "God's love, mercy, and grace," as Adam states?
- Read Leviticus 16:15-22, part of the biblical instructions for Yom Kippur, the Day of Atonement. How do the bull and two goats involved serve, in Adam's words, as expressions of remorse and gratitude to God?

- A term for the second goat, the "scapegoat," has entered everyday English language. What is a scapegoat? What examples of scapegoats, past or present, can you think of? How much or little does the modern idea reflect the biblical notion of a scapegoat?

Have participants turn in their Bibles to Hebrews. Recruit a volunteer to read aloud Hebrews 10:10-14. Discuss:

- Jesus was not descended from Aaron or belong to Levi's lineage; however, the letter to the Hebrews claims he was a priest. How does this passage say Jesus differs from other priests?
- How else does Hebrews argue that Jesus is a priest? Among other passages, see 4:14-16; 5:1-6; 7:11-28; 9:23-28. Why do you think the author considers establishing Jesus as a priest so important?
- Is it helpful for you to think of Jesus as a priest? Why or why not?
- What is the sacrifice Jesus makes? Why does the author of Hebrews say this sacrifice was necessary (10:1-4)? Why does he claim other sacrifices are no longer necessary (10:15-18)?
- Do Hebrews' claims about Jesus' superiority to the sacrifices in the Law make it an anti-semitic or anti-Jewish book? Why or why not? How can Christians affirm these claims now in ways that avoid hurtful and harmful stereotypes of Jewish people and Jewish faith?
- In 10:5-7, the author applies to Jesus Psalm 40:6-8, which belongs to a major strand of Old Testament tradition that stresses God's will more than offering sacrifices; see also 1 Samuel 15:22; Psalm 51:15-17; Jeremiah 7:1-7; Hosea 6:4-6; Micah 6:6-8. How do you and your congregation keep sacrifice and ceremony from becoming substitutes for active obedience to God?

After discussing the Scripture passages, write this heading on newsprint or markerboard: "Sacrificial Atoning Offering." Describe this atonement theory, following Adam's explanation (you may wish to write notes on the newsprint or markerboard):

- Jesus is the final, sufficient offering for humanity's sin.
- Jesus was not being punished, but offered himself to God as an atoning sacrifice.
- In his death, Jesus acted as not only the offering but also the priest making it.

Discuss:

- What does this theory tell us about human sin? About God's love?
- In your judgment, how well does this atonement theory reflect the teaching about Jesus' death found in Hebrews? Why?
- Do you think this atonement theory reflects Jesus' attitude toward forgiveness as seen in the Gospels? Why or why not?
- What implications, if any, does this atonement theory have for human offerings and sacrifices to God? To other people?

Closing Your Session

Not Mechanism, but Meaning

Remind participants that Adam encourages readers to consider Jesus' death not as a "transaction" or "mechanism" but as God's message: "Christ's death is not something *God needed* in order to forgive us, but something *we needed* in order to understand and accept that we are forgiven." Discuss:

- Do the atonement theories we've discussed today assure you of God's forgiveness? If so, how much? If not, why not?

- Both of these atonement theories attempt to balance the severity of human sin and the cost of divine forgiveness. How can over- or underemphasizing one or the other affect what we believe and how we live?
- Both these theories also affirm Jesus somehow died for us. What difference does or ought it make to believe Jesus bore our sins on his cross?
- Adam says people have asked him, "Can God really forgive me?" If someone asked you that question, how would you answer?

Closing Prayer

Sing or read aloud together "O Love Divine, What Hast Thou Done" (*The United Methodist Hymnal* #287; https://hymnary.org/text/o_love_divine_what_hast_thou_done) or another hymn or song related to this session's themes or Scriptures.

Session 3

Agnus Dei

Session Objectives

This session will help participants:

- Appreciate the nature of covenants, in Scripture and in their own experience.
- Understand the significance of the Passover lamb both within Judaism and as an image Christians use for Jesus.
- Reflect on how Jesus' institution of Holy Communion reflects and reinterprets the Passover.
- Examine what the promise of a new covenant meant in Jeremiah's time and how it can help illuminate Jesus' death.
- Consider Jesus' death as a ransom or redemption, guided by Paul's argument in Galatians 3–4.

Biblical Foundations

Then Moses called together all of Israel's elders and said to them, "Go pick out one of the flock for your families, and slaughter the Passover lamb. Take a bunch of hyssop, dip it into the blood that is in the bowl, and touch the beam above the door and the two doorposts with the blood in the bowl.

None of you should go out the door of your house until morning. When the LORD comes by to strike down the Egyptians and sees the blood on the beam above the door and on the two doorposts, the LORD will pass over that door. He won't let the destroyer enter your houses to strike you down. You should observe this ritual as a regulation for all time for you and your children. When you enter the land that the LORD has promised to give you, be sure that you observe this ritual. And when your children ask you, 'What does this ritual mean to you?' you will say, 'It is the Passover sacrifice to the LORD, for the LORD passed over the houses of the Israelites in Egypt. When he struck down the Egyptians, he spared our houses.'" The people then bowed down and worshipped.

(Exodus 12:21-27)

The time is coming, declares the LORD, when I will make a new covenant with the people of Israel and Judah. It won't be like the covenant I made with their ancestors when I took them by the hand to lead them out of the land of Egypt. They broke that covenant with me even though I was their husband, declares the LORD. No, this is the covenant that I will make with the people of Israel after that time, declares the LORD. I will put my Instructions within them and engrave them on their hearts. I will be their God, and they will be my people. They will no longer need to teach each other to say, "Know the LORD!" because they will all know me, from the least of them to the greatest, declares the LORD; for I will forgive their wrongdoing and never again remember their sins.

(Jeremiah 31:31-34)

I'm saying that as long as the heirs are minors, they are no different from slaves, though they really are the owners of everything. However, they are placed under trustees and guardians until the date set by the parents. In the same way, when we were minors, we were also enslaved by this world's system. But when the fulfillment of the time came, God sent his Son, born through a woman, and born under the Law. This was so he could redeem those under the Law so that we could be adopted. Because you are sons and daughters, God sent the Spirit of his Son into our hearts, crying, "Abba, Father!" Therefore, you are no longer a slave but a son or daughter, and if you are his child, then you are also an heir through God.

(Galatians 4:1-7)

When you were dead because of the things you had done wrong and because your body wasn't circumcised, God made you alive with Christ and forgave

all the things you had done wrong. He destroyed the record of the debt we
owed, with its requirements that worked against us. He canceled it by nail-
ing it to the cross. When he disarmed the rulers and authorities, he exposed
them to public disgrace by leading them in a triumphal parade

(Colossians 2:13-15)

Before Your Session

- Carefully and prayerfully read this session's Biblical Foundations more than once. Write down questions you have, and
try to answer them, consulting trusted Bible commentaries.
- Carefully read chapter 3 of *Why Did Jesus Have to Die?* more
than once.
- You will need: Bibles for in-person participants (*optional*: of
the same translation, for unison reading) and/or screen slides
prepared with Scripture texts for sharing (identify the translation used); newsprint or a markerboard and markers (for
in-person sessions); paper, pens or pencils (in-person).
- If using the DVD or streaming video, preview the session 3
video segment. Choose the best time in your session plan for
viewing it.
- Procure or prepare a simple wooden cross onto which
participants can nail folded pieces of paper. Alternative:
Prepare a posterboard cross onto which participants can place
sticky notes.
- *Optional*: Find a short video about the Passover seder you can
show during your session. (*Note*: Choose a video featuring
an authentic Jewish seder rather than a "Christian seder" and
that was produced by a reputable source.)

Starting Your Session

Welcome participants. Discuss:

- What's your earliest memory of someone keeping a promise to you? Of someone breaking a promise? Of a promise you made and kept or made and broke to someone else?
- Adam defines a "covenant" as "a promise or binding agreement made by one party to another, or between two parties." What are some covenants you have entered into and/or to which you've been bound in your life?
- Adam notes many covenants include "an outward and visible sign of the agreement." What covenantal signs are you familiar with in your life?
- Adam states the word *covenant* occurs more than 350 times in Scripture. What biblical covenants can you name? (List responses on newsprint or markerboard.)

Tell participants that in this session, your group will explore some ways Scripture uses the language of promise and covenant to present the meaning and significance of Jesus' death.

Opening Prayer

Faithful God, through the ages you have made and kept promises to your people and to the world. We gather now trusting in your promise to send your Spirit when we read and study the Scriptures in dependence upon you. Help us trace the story of your constant, covenant love, that we may more fully embrace life as your covenant people. We make our prayer in the name of your Son, Jesus Christ, in whom every one of your promises is "Yes" and "Amen," to your glory.

Watch Session Video

Watch the session 3 video segment together. Discuss:

- Which of Adam's statements most interested, intrigued, surprised, or confused you? Why?
- What questions does this video segment raise for you?

Book Discussion Questions

The Promise of the Passover Lamb

Tell participants the Jewish festival of Passover is the annual celebration of God liberating the Hebrew people from slavery in Egypt.

Optional: Show the Passover seder video you selected before your session. Ask any participants who have attended a Passover seder to talk briefly about their experiences.

Discuss:

- The Passover seder, as Adam describes, is "food, ritual, and storytelling" designed to help people see themselves in the "defining story" of the Exodus. What are the "defining stories" of your life? How did you first learn them? How do you keep these stories alive?

Have participants turn in their Bibles to Exodus. Recruit a volunteer to read aloud Exodus 12:21-27. Discuss:

- What promise from God is connected to the Passover lamb?
- Why does God command the people to "observe this ritual as a regulation for all time" (v. 24)?
- What ritua observances have you explained to children, as God instructs the people to explain the Passover lamb (vv. 26-27)? How can such explanations make ritual observances and the "defining stories" they recall more meaningful for both children and adults?
- How is the story of Jesus' death a "defining story" for Christians? How is it like and unlike the story of the Passover?
- How is Jesus like and unlike the Passover lamb?
- How is Holy Communion (the Lord's Supper; the Eucharist) like and unlike the Passover seder? What promises are connected with Communion?

- When, if ever, has Communion especially helped you see yourself in the "defining story" of Jesus' death?
- How helpful or meaningful do you find the image of Jesus as Passover lamb and why?

A New Covenant

Recruit a volunteer to read aloud Jeremiah 31:31-34. Discuss:

- What covenant did God make with God's people at the time of the Exodus? What promises and agreements did it contain? (See also: Exodus 19:1-8; 20:1-17; Deuteronomy 30:15-20.)
- Read Exodus 24:3-8. What is the physical sign of God's covenant with the people at Mount Sinai?
- Through Jeremiah, God says the people broke the covenant (v. 32). How so?
- As Adam notes, the Bible frequently depicts covenant relationship between God and humanity as a marriage. How is the broken covenant like and unlike a broken marriage?
- What does God promise to do about the broken covenant (v. 33)? What will the results of God's actions be (v. 34)?
- Read 1 Corinthians 11:23-25; Mark 14:22-24; Matthew 26:26-28; and Luke 22:19-20. How do these connect Jesus' death to the covenant made at Sinai and/or to the "new covenant" announced in Jeremiah?
- How helpful or meaningful do you find the concept of covenant for understanding Jesus' death and why?

Ransom and Redemption

Write the words "ransom" and "redemption" on newsprint or markerboard. Ask volunteers to define the words, then explain, as Adam does, that the two words can be synonymous and in the ancient world could refer to the cost of buying something back, especially the freedom of enslaved people.

Have participants turn in their Bibles to Galatians. Recruit a volunteer to read aloud Galatians 4:1-7. Discuss:

- Why does Paul say heirs who are minors are no different than people who are enslaved (vv. 1-2)? How does Paul apply this situation to believers' situation before Christ (v. 3) and after Christ (vv. 4-7)?

- This passage is part of a larger—and, as Adam notes, "confusing" to many—argument. Read Galatians 3:1-13. What mistake about their experience of God does Paul think his readers in Galatia are making? What is "the curse of the Law" and how does Christ redeem people from it, according to Paul?

- Paul affirmed the Law as God's good gift (for example, Romans 7:12-13; 9:4-5), but had come to experience it, Adam believes, as "a kind of spiritual enslavement." When, if ever, have you known or know of Christians who treat God's good gifts as occasions for enslavement? How can we recognize and reject the temptation to do so?

- In Galatians 4:3, Paul refers to having been enslaved "by this world's system" rather than the Law. What is he talking about? How, if at all, might enslavement to the Law and "this world's system" be related?

- Read Mark 10:41-45. Why did Jesus say he would give his life as "a ransom for many" (v. 45 NRSV)?

- Adam says some Christians have held that "Jesus gave his life as a ransom [for us] to the devil," but that this idea is an example of treating Jesus' words "literally and transactionally, and not figuratively or metaphorically." What do you think?

- Adam suggests Jesus' death "has 'bought out' or 'paid in full' the old contract of the Law, so that we might live under a new covenant or contract." If so, what role, if any, does or ought the Law play in Christians' lives?

- How helpful do you find the ransom or redemption theory of the atonement?

Closing Your Session

Canceling the Cheirographon

Read aloud Colossians 2:13-15. Read aloud from Adam's book: "There is just one Greek word behind the phrase, 'the record of the debt we owed'—the Greek word *cheirographon.* . . . [It means] contracts or IOUs signed with terms of repayment and also receipts when payment was made. . . . Paul imagines a list of all the sins we have committed, seeing them as debts that are owed. . . . This list of debts was . . . nailed to the cross."

Distribute small pieces of scrap paper or blank sticky notes to participants. Invite them to write not a list of all their sins but simply one. Promise them no one else will read their note. When participants are ready, invite them to come forward and nail their *cheirographon* to a wooden cross (as Adam's congregation did), or to stick their sticky notes to a posterboard cross.

Closing Prayer

Sing or read aloud together "This Is the Feast of Victory" (*The United Methodist Hymnal* #638; https://hymnary.org/text/worthy_is_christ _the_lamb_who_was) or another hymn or song related to this session's themes or scriptures.

Session 4

Were You There

Session Objectives

This session will help participants:

- Reflect on *The Crucifixion* by Léonard Limosin as an image of moral theories of the atonement.
- Consider selfishness as humanity's "original sin" from which Jesus came to save us.
- Explore Jesus' teaching about living a "cruciform life" in Matthew 16:24-26.
- Understand the basic elements of the moral influence (or moral example) theory of the atonement.
- Ponder Jesus' washing of his disciples' feet (John 13) as an example of the humble, selfless service to which he calls his followers.
- Identify specific ways in which they are or could be serving others.

Biblical Foundations

One of the criminals hanging next to Jesus insulted him: "Aren't you the Christ? Save yourself and us!"

Responding, the other criminal spoke harshly to him, "Don't you fear God, seeing that you've also been sentenced to die? We are rightly condemned, for we are receiving the appropriate sentence for what we did. But this man has done nothing wrong." Then he said, "Jesus, remember me when you come into your kingdom."

Jesus replied, "I assure you that today you will be with me in paradise."
(Luke 23:39-43)

Then Jesus said to his disciples, "All who want to come after me must say no to themselves, take up their cross, and follow me. All who want to save their lives will lose them. But all who lose their lives because of me will find them. Why would people gain the whole world but lose their lives? What will people give in exchange for their lives?"
(Matthew 16:24-26)

After [Jesus] washed the disciples' feet, he put on his robes and returned to his place at the table. He said to them, "Do you know what I've done for you? You call me 'Teacher' and 'Lord,' and you speak correctly, because I am. If I, your Lord and teacher, have washed your feet, you too must wash each other's feet. I have given you an example: Just as I have done, you also must do. I assure you, servants aren't greater than their master, nor are those who are sent greater than the one who sent them. Since you know these things, you will be happy if you do them."
(John 13:12-17)

Before Your Session

- Carefully and prayerfully read this session's Biblical Foundations more than once. Write down questions you have, and try to answer them, consulting trusted Bible commentaries.
- Carefully read chapter 4 of *Why Did Jesus Have to Die?* more than once.
- You will need: Bibles for in-person participants (*optional*: of the same translation, for unison reading) and/or screen slides prepared with Scripture texts for sharing (identify the translation used); newsprint or a markerboard and markers (for in-person sessions); paper, pens or pencils (in-person).

- If using the DVD or streaming video, preview the session 4 video segment. Choose the best time in your session plan for viewing it.

- Locate an online image of *The Crucifixion* by Léonard Limosin that you can project for in-person participants and/or show via screen sharing to remote participants. The painting is also reproduced in Adam's book.

Starting Your Session

Welcome participants. Display the image of *The Crucifixion* by Léonard Limosin you located before your session, and/or encourage participants to look at the painting as reproduced in Adam's book. Discuss:

- What detail(s) do you notice first when you look at this painting?

- What detail(s) in this painting most intrigue you? Confuse you? Why?

- Who are the people around the cross in this painting? What does their presence suggest about the significance of Jesus' death?

- Adam points out that, in the painting, "the dividing line between light and darkness is the crucified Christ." What significance do you find in this division?

- Adam describes the painting's depiction of two castles and two warring armies. What does this imagery suggest in the context of the Crucifixion?

- Adam notes the skull beneath the cross that represents Adam. How does this detail connect with the recapitulation theory of the atonement (discussed in session 1)?

- Adam states that the book beneath the skull "represents the Torah or the first covenant." How does this detail connect with the new covenant theory of the atonement (discussed in session 3)?
- What do you see above the heads of the thieves crucified alongside Jesus? What do these details mean?
- Why do you think the artist includes himself among those standing at the foot of Jesus' cross?
- What other thoughts and/or feelings does this painting spark for you? Why?

Tell participants that Adam says Limosin's painting "illustrates multiple theories of the atonement," but primarily illustrates "the moral theory of the atonement," a subjective theory that invites us to consider our own response to Jesus' death.

Opening Prayer

Loving God, we confess we do not always stand before Jesus' cross with the attention, the penitence, and the devotion he is due. Too often, it is nothing to we who pass by, wrapped up in our concerns, busy with our lives. In this time of study, may your Spirit bring us again, in mind and heart, to that holy ground where Jesus died, that we may more fully worship him who died to save us from our sins, and to empower us for lives of loving service. Amen.

Watch Session Video

Watch the session 4 video segment together. Discuss:

- Which of Adam's statements most interested, intrigued, surprised, or confused you? Why?
- What questions does this video segment raise for you?

Book Discussion Questions

Original Selfishness

Discuss:

- Adam argues that selfishness is ultimately "the source of our pain and the pain we inflict on one another." Do you agree? Why or why not?
- Adam discusses objectivism, the philosophy espoused by Ayn Rand that "identified selfishness as a virtue." How do you react to this philosophy? When and how do you see people treating selfishness as a virtue? When are you aware of this tendency in yourself?
- Adam also discusses evolutionary biologist Richard Dawkins's identification of a "selfish gene": "Unlike [Ayn] Rand, Dawkins wasn't advocating for selfishness, merely recognizing the reality and the importance of overcoming this biological predisposition." Do you think, as Adam says, selfishness is "hardwired" into humanity? What role might it have played in human evolution? Does a biological basis for selfishness ever justify or excuse selfish behavior? Why or why not?
- According to Adam, "Howard University paleobiologist and anatomy professor Daryl Domning and Georgetown theology professor Monika Helwig . . . suggested that selfishness is a significant link between the Bible's creation story and evolutionary theory." How is the biblical story of Adam and Eve in Eden (Genesis 3) a story about selfishness?
- What might we gain and/or lose, if anything, by thinking about selfishness as our "original sin"?

The Cruciform Life

Have participants turn in their Bibles to Matthew 16. Recruit a volunteer to read aloud Matthew 16:24-26. Discuss:

- *"Jesus came,"* writes Adam, *"not merely to forgive sin, but to save us from it."* What is the distinction between the two? How important a distinction is it, and why?
- What does it mean, practically, to deny one's self and "take up [the] cross" (v. 24)?
- How does losing life for Jesus' sake lead to finding life (v. 25)?
- Are Jesus' words in verse 26 a warning about selfishness? If so, how? If not, why not?
- How does Jesus and Peter's exchange before these verses (in 16:21-23) help us understand the life to which Jesus calls his followers?
- How would you answer criticisms that Jesus' teaching about the importance of self-denial can lead people to make unhealthy or even self-destructive choices?
- Adam writes that Jesus' death "was the climax of his entire life of selfless service rather than selfish self-centeredness." What else do you know about Jesus' life that exemplifies his selfless service?
- Adam mentions scientific research into positive health outcomes associated with selflessness behavior, such as volunteerism. What positive outcomes, health-related or otherwise, have you and/or those you know experienced from selfless living? How relevant do you think these benefits are to Jesus' call to cruciform living, and why?
- Adam calls "lives shaped by selflessness and sacrifice" cruciform (cross-shaped) lives. Who are some people you know or know of whom you would say live cruciform lives? Why?

Moral Influence (or Moral Example) Theory of the Atonement

Write the heading "Moral Influence (or Moral Example) Theory" on newsprint or markerboard. Write notes summarizing Adam's explanation of this theory:

- Jesus came "to *change us* so that we might resist our internal urge to sin," and died "to *show us the way* and *to move us to change.*"
- Jesus died as a moral exemplar, "to move our hearts by his death so that we feel compelled to follow" him.
- The moral theories of atonement are "subjective" because, rather than focusing on any objective differences Jesus' death makes, "they explain Christ's death in terms of its subjective or emotional impact on the hearts of those who believe."
- "The moral influence and moral example theories . . . do not replace the other theories but add to them."

Discuss:

- What do you think about these moral theories of the atonement?
- Read these: Galatians 2:20; Ephesians 5:1-2; Philippians 2:3-8. To what extent do these Scripture passages support moral theories of the atonement?
- What questions raised by the objective atonement theories, if any, do the subjective theories resolve?
- What questions, if any, about the meaning and significance of Jesus' death do subjective atonement theories leave unresolved?

"I Have Given You an Example"

Have participants turn in their Bibles to John 13. Recruit a volunteer to read aloud John 13:12-17. Discuss:

- Why has Jesus washed his disciples' feet (vv. 14-15; see also 13:1, 8b)?
- Why was this action a surprising one for Jesus to do? (see also 13:8a)

- Adam states that Jesus' actions are "a foreshadowing of what he would do the next day" in his death. How so?

- What does Jesus promise his disciples about following his example (v. 17; see also vv. 34-35)?

- Adam quotes the late Pope Francis's explanation of foot washing's significance: "Love isn't words, but works and service, humble service." When have you seen and/or taken part in works of humble service you believe communicated God's love?

- "Even completely nonreligious people are often moved when they see Christians and churches selflessly serving others," Adam writes. When, if ever, have you seen this reaction in your experience?

- Some Christian traditions include foot washing as part of their worship, especially on Maundy (or Holy) Thursday. Have you ever experienced a foot washing service? If so, what was it like? If not, would you want to? Does your congregation practice foot washing? Why or why not?

- As Adam states, "Many people are uncomfortable having their feet examined by their friends, much less strangers." What other ritual practices, if any, might communicate the message of foot washing, and why? How important is it for congregations to include foot washing or something analogous to it in their worship, and why?

Closing Your Session

The Most Urgent Question

Tell participants that Adam quotes Dr. Martin Luther King Jr.'s comment that the "most persistent and urgent question" in life is "What are you doing for others?"

Distribute scrap paper. Invite participants to make notes about how they would answer this question. Emphasize that you will not ask or expect participants to show their notes to anyone else, and that the point of this activity is not to compose a list of "bragging points," but to take stock of how they think and feel about the extent they are, or could be, serving others.

After two to three minutes, read aloud from Adam's book: "[Jesus] didn't just tell others to deny themselves and take up their crosses. He demonstrated this self-denial himself." What would our world look like if all of us who claim to follow Jesus actually denied ourselves, took up our crosses, and followed him?"

Closing Prayer

Sing or read aloud together "Were You There" (*The United Methodist Hymnal* #288; https://hymnary.org/text/were_you_there _when_they_crucified_my_lo) or another hymn or song related to this session's themes or Scripture passages.

SESSION 5

WHAT WONDROUS
LOVE IS THIS

Session Objectives

This session will help participants:

*   Reflect on expressions of love they find meaningful.
*   Consider John 3:16 as a possible summary of the gospel in the context of both the Old Testament's and Jesus' own witness to God's love.
*   Think about Jesus' death as God's own expression of the self-sacrificial love Jesus commands of his followers in John 15.
*   Discuss the significance of the cross as a sign in church and society.

Biblical Foundations

No one has gone up to heaven except the one who came down from heaven, the Human One. Just as Moses lifted up the snake in the wilderness, so must the Human One be lifted up so that everyone who believes in him will have eternal life. God so loved the world that he gave his only Son, so that everyone who believes in him won't perish but will have eternal life. God didn't send his Son into the world to judge the world, but that the world might be saved through him.

(John 3:13-17)

[Jesus said,] "As the Father loved me, I too have loved you. Remain in my love. If you keep my commandments, you will remain in my love, just as I kept my Father's commandments and remain in his love. I have said these things to you so that my joy will be in you and your joy will be complete. This is my commandment: love each other just as I have loved you. No one has greater love than to give up one's life for one's friends. You are my friends if you do what I command you. I don't call you servants any longer, because servants don't know what their master is doing. Instead, I call you friends, because everything I heard from my Father I have made known to you. You didn't choose me, but I chose you and appointed you so that you could go and produce fruit and so that your fruit could last. As a result, whatever you ask the Father in my name, he will give you. I give you these commandments so that you can love each other."

(John 15:9-17)

Dear friends, let's love each other, because love is from God, and everyone who loves is born from God and knows God. The person who doesn't love does not know God, because God is love. This is how the love of God is revealed to us: God has sent his only Son into the world so that we can live through him. This is love: it is not that we loved God but that he loved us and sent his Son as the sacrifice that deals with our sins.

Dear friends, if God loved us this way, we also ought to love each other.

(1 John 4:7-11)

Before Your Session

- Carefully and prayerfully read this session's Biblical Foundations more than once. Write down questions you have and try to answer them, consulting trusted Bible commentaries.
- Carefully read chapter 5 of *Why Did Jesus Have to Die?* more than once.
- You will need: Bibles for in-person participants (*optional*: of the same translation, for unison reading) and/or screen slides

prepared with Scripture texts for sharing (identify the translation used); newsprint or a markerboard and markers (for in-person sessions); paper, pens or pencils (in-person).

- If using the DVD or streaming video, preview the session 5 video segment. Choose the best time in your session plan for viewing it.

- *Optional*: Find an image of the Helzberg Diamonds' "I Am Loved" button online to display during your session.

Starting Your Session

Welcome participants. Read aloud from Adam's book: "In 1967, [jewelry store CEO Barnett Helzberg Jr.] had an idea: when romantic partners or spouses give jewelry, it is a way of saying to someone, 'You are loved.' . . . Yet he recognized not everyone can afford jewelry, so Helzberg had buttons printed up that said, 'I Am Loved.' . . . [Helzberg's stores have] given away over fifty million of these iconic buttons." *Optional*: Display an image of the buttons, as found in Adam's book and/or online. Discuss:

- Do you or would you wear an "I Am Loved" button? Why or why not?

- What physical gift have you received that most communicated the giver's love for you, and why?

- What's one memorable gift you've given someone to show you love them? How was your gift received?

- What everyday expressions of love mean the most to you? Why?

- Barnett Helzberg told Adam, "Everyone wants to be loved." Is he right? Why or why not?

Tell participants that, in this session, your group will consider Jesus' death as, in Adam's words, "the ultimate expression of God's selfless and sacrificial love for humanity."

Opening Prayer

God of gods and Ruler of rulers, we give you thanks because your faithful love endures forever. In love, you made the heavens and earth and gave us your good garden as our home. In love, you liberated from slavery the people you chose as a light to the nations. In love, you came among us in your Son Jesus, who gave himself for the life of the world. May we sense your Spirit surrounding us now, that we may more deeply know your eternal and faithful love, and may be made more ready to share it with all. Amen.

Watch Session Video

Watch the session 5 video segment together. Discuss:

- Which of Adam's statements most interested, intrigued, surprised, or confused you? Why?
- What questions does this video segment raise for you?

Book Discussion Questions

John 3:16 and the Character of God

Have participants turn in their Bible to John 3. Recruit a volunteer to read aloud 3:13-17. (If time allows, recruit three volunteers to read aloud 3:1-18 as the narrator, Nicodemus, and Jesus.) Discuss:

- How do these verses' context (see 3:1-12) help us understand why Jesus stresses his authority to speak "about heavenly things" (v. 12)? What does he say is the basis of this authority (v. 13)?
- What is Jesus talking about in verses 14-15? Why does he compare it to the bronze serpent Moses made (Numbers 21:4-9)?

- Why has verse 16 become, as Adam says, "perhaps the most famous passage of Scripture"? Do you think John 3:16 is, as Martin Luther called it, "the gospel in miniature"? Do you or would you use it to summarize the gospel for other people? Why or why not?

- "Jesus devoted his life and ministry to seeking out those who were made to feel unloved by God," Adam tells us. What stories from the Gospels can you remember or locate that illustrate Jesus' "mercy, compassion, and love . . . to the broken, the hurting, and those far from God"?

- Adam says people sometimes ask him, "Why is God so angry in the Old Testament and so loving in the New Testament?" How would you answer this question? Why do you think this question is a common one? When, if ever, have you asked it?

- Read Psalm 136 and Lamentations 3:22-23. As Adam explains, the Hebrew word translated "faithful love" (verse 22, CEB; "steadfast love," NRSV), *hesed*, occurs nearly 250 times in the Old Testament. (Optional: Use an online or print concordance to find other occurrences.) What is God's *hesed* like, according to these and other Scriptures?

- Adam also states that the Hebrew word *ahav*, signaling affectionate love, occurs more than two hundred times in the Old Testament. Read Jeremiah 31:2-3 and Hosea 11:1-4. What is the love of God like, according to these scriptures?

- According to Adam, some (not all) religious leaders in Jesus' time, "like many today, . . . saw God more like a judge, harsh critic, or a strict or angry parent" than as loving. Do you most often think of God as strict and angry, or loving and forgiving? Why? How, if at all, have your thoughts about the character of God changed over time?

- "In a sense, [Jesus'] entire life and ministry was about atonement—he was constantly seeking to reconcile people to

God." Does this view of Jesus' life make his death seem more or less important? If so, why? If not, why not?

- How can and do your congregation seek to reconcile people to God?

No Greater Love

Summarize the true-life stories Adam tells about people who sacrificed their lives for others, and/or relate such a story of your own. Invite participants to briefly talk about people they have known or known of who have sacrificed their lives for others.

Have participants turn to John 15 in their Bibles. Recruit a volunteer to read aloud John 15:12-17. Discuss:

- What commandment does Jesus give his disciples and why?
- What does obeying this command look like practically and concretely?
- How does Jesus' definition and example of love confirm and/or challenge other understandings of love?
- Why does Jesus teach that self-sacrifice for friends is the greatest love (v. 13)?
- Adam writes, "I've wondered what impact it would have on me if a parent or friend or stranger died for me?" What impact do you imagine such a death would have—or, perhaps, has had—on you?
- Does Jesus command all his followers to demonstrate self-sacrificial love? Why or why not? Can a person love self-sacrificially without giving up their life? If so, how? If not, why not?
- What are some selfless acts of love others have performed for you? How have those actions shaped your life?
- Adam asks, "What differentiates Jesus' death on the cross from [other] remarkable acts of love and sacrifice?" How would you answer that question?

- Read Romans 5:6-8. What does Paul teach here about the significance of Jesus' death? How does this teaching relate to Jesus' words about great love in John 13?
- What is the link between obedience and love with God and Jesus (John 15:9)? Between obedience and friendship with Jesus (v. 14)? Do you think such statements make divine love and friendship conditional? Why or why not?
- What is the difference between being Jesus' "servant" (the Greek word can also be translated "slave") and being Jesus' friend (v. 15)? Do you consider yourself Jesus' servant (slave) or friend? Both? Neither? Why?
- Why does Jesus stress that he chose his followers, not vice versa (v. 16)? What difference, if any, does this distinction make to you as you follow Jesus?
- What is the everlasting "fruit" Jesus chose for his followers to produce? What evidence of this fruit do you see in your congregation's life? In your own?
- When was a time, if ever, you sensed you were remaining in Jesus' love?

Closing Your Session

The Wondrous Cross

Read aloud from Adam's book: "For Christians, the cross is God's way of saying to us, 'You are loved.' This is, in part, why Christians wear crosses—to signify they know they are loved by God. The practice of wearing crosses also. . . . reflects one's decision to follow a crucified king, and to live a life of sacrificial love in response to his death for us."

Recruit a volunteer to read aloud 1 John 4:7-11. Discuss:

- What does this Scripture passage tell us about the significance of Jesus' death? What ethical implications does it draw from Jesus' death?

- What is John's criterion for identifying who knows God? Do you agree with it? Why or why not?
- Do you choose to wear a cross? Why or why not?
- In your experience, how, if at all, do people outside the church react differently to the cross as a symbol than people inside the church?
- Do you think the cross remains a powerful sign of God's love in society today? Why or why not?
- How might your everyday life be different if everyone who looked at you could plainly see a cross on your person?

Closing Prayer

Sing or read aloud together "What Wondrous Love Is This" (*The United Methodist Hymnal* #292; https://hymnary.org/text/what _wondrous_love_is_this_o_my_soul_o_m) or another hymn or song related to this session's themes or Scriptures.

SESSION 6

CHRIST THE LORD IS RISEN TODAY

Session Objectives

This session will help participants:

- Reflect on reasons that the battle between good and evil is such a common theme in human stories.
- Understand and articulate basic elements of the *Christus Victor* theory of the atonement.
- Consider what Hebrews 2 teaches about the purpose of Jesus' death in light of the *Christus Victor* theory.
- Consider Jesus' teaching about his death in John 12 as teaching about his "strategic plan" for changing the world.
- Review new insights they have gained during this study into the significance of Jesus' death.

Biblical Foundations

Therefore, since the children share in flesh and blood, [Jesus] also shared the same things in the same way. He did this to destroy the one who holds the power over death—the devil—by dying. He set free those who were held in slavery their entire lives by their fear of death. Of course, he isn't trying to help angels, but rather he's helping Abraham's descendants. Therefore, he had to be made like his brothers and sisters in every way. This was so that he could become a merciful and faithful high priest in things relating to God, in order to wipe away the sins of the people. He's able to help those who are being tempted, since he himself experienced suffering when he was tempted.

(Hebrews 2:14-18)

Jesus replied, "The time has come for the Human One to be glorified. I assure you that unless a grain of wheat falls into the earth and dies, it can only be a single seed. But if it dies, it bears much fruit. Those who love their lives will lose them, and those who hate their lives in this world will keep them forever. Whoever serves me must follow me. Wherever I am, there my servant will also be. My Father will honor whoever serves me."

(John 12:23-26)

This is what I'm saying, brothers and sisters: Flesh and blood can't inherit God's kingdom. Something that rots can't inherit something that doesn't decay. Listen, I'm telling you a secret: All of us won't die, but we will all be changed—in an instant, in the blink of an eye, at the final trumpet. The trumpet will blast, and the dead will be raised with bodies that won't decay, and we will be changed. It's necessary for this rotting body to be clothed with what can't decay, and for the body that is dying to be clothed in what can't die. And when the rotting body has been clothed in what can't decay, and the dying body has been clothed in what can't die, then this statement in scripture will happen:

> Death has been swallowed up by a victory.
> Where is your victory, Death?
> Where is your sting, Death?

(1 Corinthians 15:50-55)

Before Your Session

- Carefully and prayerfully read this session's Biblical Foundations more than once. Write down questions you have, and try to answer them, consulting trusted Bible commentaries.

- Carefully read chapter 6 and the Postscript of *Why Did Jesus Have to Die?* more than once.
- You will need: Bibles for in-person participants (*optional*: of the same translation, for unison reading) and/or screen slides prepared with Scripture texts for sharing (identify the translation used); newsprint or a markerboard and markers (for in-person sessions); paper, pens or pencils (in-person).
- If using the DVD or streaming video, preview the session 6 video segment. Choose the best time in your session plan for viewing it.

Starting Your Session

Welcome participants. Invite volunteers to talk briefly about their favorite stories of a battle between good and evil from movies and TV, theater, games, or literature. Discuss:

- Why do you think the battle between good and evil is such a common focus of the stories we human beings tell?
- Are all stories in which good wins this battle good stories? Are all stories in which evil wins this battle bad stories? Why?
- When and where have you seen good winning a victory over evil in the world? In your society? In your own life? What about evil winning a victory over good?
- Adam quotes Alexander Solzhenitsyn's claim that "the line dividing good and evil cuts through the heart of every human being." Do these words seem true to you? Why or why not?

Tell participants that, in this last session together, your group will consider one last theory of the atonement, which, in Adam's words, "sees the meaning of the Crucifixion and Resurrection in the light of the epic battle between light and darkness, good and evil, love and hate, God and the demonic powers."

Opening Prayer

Great and amazing are your deeds, Lord God Almighty! Righteous and true are your ways, Ruler of all! Through the ages, you have won many battles over sin, evil, and death; and in the dying and rising of your Son, Jesus Christ, you reveal your ultimate triumph over all that opposes your good will. As we gather to study and pray, still waiting for the full and final manifestation of your victory, may your Spirit help us trust your power, know your presence, and share your peace. Amen.

Watch Session Video

Watch the session 6 video segment together. Discuss:

- Which of Adam's statements most interested, intrigued, surprised, or confused you? Why?
- What questions does this video segment raise for you?

Book Discussion Questions

The Battle Between Good and Evil

Discuss:

- "Most people in the time of Jesus," writes Adam, "believed there were spiritual forces that sought to lure humans away from what is right and good." Do you share this belief? Why or why not?
- Read Ephesians 6:12. What does this say about spiritual forces of evil? How does or how ought its teaching shape our view of those we consider enemies?
- Does believing in spiritual forces of evil help us understand the world and ourselves more or less? Does this belief increase or decrease human responsibility against evil? Why?

- What stories from the Gospels can you remember or find about Jesus confronting demonic powers and spiritual forces of evil? Why did Jesus' followers remember and pass on these stories? How important or unimportant are these stories to your understanding of and faith in Jesus? Why?

- As Adam notes, although the Gospels mention Satan prompting Judas to betray Jesus (Luke 22:3-4; John 13:2), they do not mention Satan in connection with Jesus' crucifixion itself. What, if anything, do you think this omission means? Do you see evidence of spiritual evil in the evil "politicians, 'peacekeepers,' and preachers" commit? Why or why not?

Christ the Victorious

Write the heading "*Christus Victor*" on newsprint or markerboard. Summarize Adam's explanation of this atonement theory:

- The early church saw Jesus' death as an "epic battle" against "principalities and powers, earthly and demonic."
- In Jesus' crucifixion, evil appears to have won, but in his resurrection, Christ emerges victorious over evil.
- Jesus did not destroy sin and evil, but "clearly demonstrated his power over them."
- This theory is called *Christus Victor*, Latin for "Christ the Victor" or "Christ the Victorious."
- Lutheran bishop and theologian Gustaf Aulén wrote an influential book about this theory, *Christus Victor* (1931), calling it "the ruling idea of the Atonement for the first thousand years of Christian history."

Have participants turn in their Bibles to Hebrews 2. Recruit a volunteer to read aloud Hebrews 2:14-18. Discuss:

- According to this, why did Jesus share humanity's "flesh and blood" (v. 14), and why did Jesus die?

- Who are Jesus' "brothers and sisters" (v. 17) in this Scripture passage, and what benefits do they receive from Jesus' death?
- Does this Scripture text support a *Christus Victor* theory of the atonement? Why or why not? What other atonement theories, if any, do you recognize in this Scripture?
- Read 1 John 3:8 and Colossians 2:15. Do these Scripture texts support the *Christus Victor* atonement theory? Why or why not?
- How helpful or unhelpful do you find the *Christus Victor* theory in understanding the meaning of Jesus' death? Why?

Living a Resurrection Life

Have participants turn in their Bibles to John 12. Recruit a volunteer to read aloud John 12:23-26. Discuss:

- In John's Gospel, Jesus' crucifixion is the time of his glorification. Based on these verses, how is Jesus, "the Human One" (v. 23; "Son of Man," NRSV) glorified in his death?
- Why does Jesus use the analogy of planted wheat grain (v. 24) to talk about his death's significance?
- What does Jesus mean by loving and hating life in this world (v. 25)? What does such love and hate look like, specifically and concretely?
- What expectation does Jesus hold for those who serve him, and what promise does he hold out to them (v. 26)?
- How would you answer someone who asked, "Why does Jesus want me to hate my life? Why does Christianity want me to value some next life over this one?"
- Adam says these verses express Jesus' "strategic plan for how God's kingdom comes" and his "strategic plan for changing the world." What does this plan show us about Jesus? About God? About Jesus' disciples, then and now?

- Adam invites readers to consider how many people they might influence for good over the course of their lives. Who is one person you believe you have influenced for good? How did you do so? How has or might Jesus use that influence as part of his "strategic plan" for changing the world?
- "One of the joys of being a part of a church is that you can do things together you could not do alone." If you are part of a congregation, what are some things you do with them to serve Jesus and influence others for good that you could not do on your own?
- How, if at all, might Jesus' "strategic plan" connect with the *Christus Victor* theory of the atonement?

Counting on the Resurrection

Have participants turn their Bibles to 1 Corinthians 15. Tell them Paul spends this entire chapter discussing belief in the resurrection of the dead, of whom Jesus is the first to be raised. Invite participants to spend a few minutes reading or skimming the chapter, then ask volunteers to identify some of what they think are the most interesting or important points Paul makes about resurrection. Write responses on newsprint or markerboard.

Recruit a volunteer to read aloud 1 Corinthians 15:50-55. Discuss:

- What is the "secret" Paul tells in these verses?
- What does this secret make you think? How does it make you feel?
- How might Paul's description of our resurrection connect with the *Christus Victor* theory of the atonement (vv. 54-55)?
- Adam writes that when he visits people who are dying and their families, he will read such scriptures as John 14:1-3 and John 11:25-26. Read these passages. How have you or how do you think you might respond to them in such circumstances, and why?

- What Scripture verses help you think about the deaths of your loved ones? About your own inevitable death? Why?
- "The death and resurrection of Christ does not eliminate all of our fears or grief in the face of death. But it does allow us to grieve and face death as those who have hope." Do you agree? Why or why not?
- What's the difference between "believing in" the resurrection of the dead and "counting on" it, as Adam told his friend Chuck he is counting on it? Would you say you are "counting on" the resurrection? Why or why not?

Closing Your Session

What Is God Trying to Say to You?

Remind participants of each of the atonement theories Adam discusses and your group has learned about over the course of this study (you may wish to write them on newsprint or markerboard as you do):

- The Crucifixion as God's Word—Jesus' death is a message from God.
- Recapitulation—Jesus becomes a "new Adam," reversing the events in Eden.
- Penal Substitution—Jesus bears the punishment for our sin.
- Sacrificial Offering for Sin—Jesus offers himself for our forgiveness.
- Christ as Passover Lamb—Jesus delivers humanity from slavery and death.
- New Covenant—Jesus initiates a new covenant by his blood.
- Ransom—Jesus gives his life to ransom us from the evil one.
- Redemption—Jesus purchases our freedom from sin and judgment.
- Moral Influence and Moral Example—Jesus' death leads us to repentance and is an example of love for us to follow.

- *Christus Victor*—By his death, Jesus defeats death and the forces of evil.

Discuss:

- Which of these atonement theories did you find most meaningful, and why?
- What new ideas about Jesus' death do you have as a result of our study?
- What questions about Jesus' death do you still have? How will you seek answers?
- Throughout this book, Adam has encouraged us to see Jesus' death not as a transaction, but as a communication from God. What do you believe God is trying to say to you through Jesus' death?

Read aloud from Adam's book: "The benefits of Christ's Passion are given as a gift. We don't earn them. We don't deserve them. We simply accept them. We trust in the crucified and resurrected Christ."

Thank group members for participating in this study. If you have not already, make plans for your group's next study.

Closing Prayer

Sing or read aloud together "Christ the Lord Is Risen Today" (*The United Methodist Hymnal* #302; https://hymnary.org/text/christ_the _lord_is_risen_today_wesley) or another hymn or song related to this session's themes or scriptures.

Coming April 21, 2026

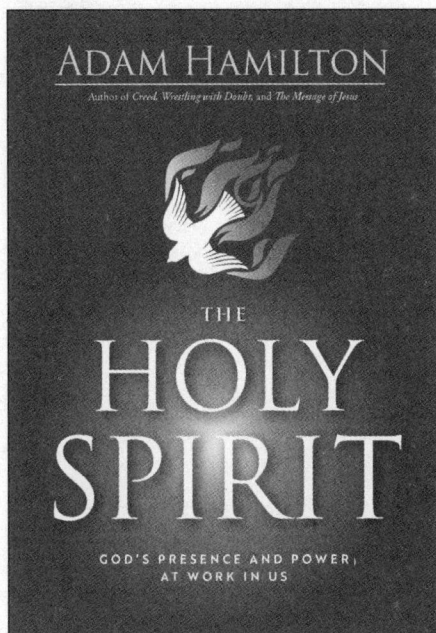

The Holy Spirit is God's active presence and power at work in the world. It is the Holy Spirit that transforms, leads, empowers, and guides us. Jesus spoke of the Spirit as one who comes alongside his followers to comfort and counsel us. He said the Spirit would empower and work in his followers to transform the world. The entire Christian life and experience is dependent on the Holy Spirit's presence and power.

In *The Holy Spirit*, Adam Hamilton traces the Bible's teaching about the Holy Spirit in the Hebrew Bible, Jesus' promises concerning the Spirit in the Gospels, the Pentecostal experience of the Holy Spirit in the Acts of the Apostles, and finally, the teachings New Testament epistles concerning the Spirit's work in the lives of believers.

Free small-group discussion guide
and streaming videos available.

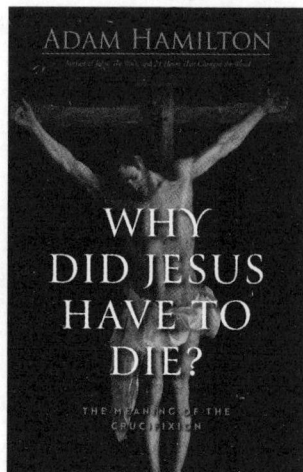